The Complete Guide to Gardeners

The Plant Obsessed
and How to Deal With Them

Written and illustrated by

Joseph Tychonievich

Dedicated
with love and gratitude
to my long suffering husband.

Table of Contents

Introduction

This book is written for everyone who has a gardener in their life. Perhaps you are dating a gardener or are already married to one. Perhaps you realize now that your dear child, for whom you had such dreams, is not a computer nerd, or a musician, or a doctor, or anything you had hoped, but, in fact, a gardener. Perhaps you know someone who, for years, was seemingly perfectly normal and sane, and then one year they decided to grow a few tomatoes, the next year a few more, and now, suddenly, all they can talk or think about is tomatoes. Sometimes it comes on suddenly like that. Sometimes they've been that way all their life. Whoever they are, and however their gardening developed, know that you are not alone. Gardening is a widespread, debilitating condition.

Discovering their child is a gardener.

I've known gardeners who are famous academics, writing important dense works of feminist theory when not weeding their impressive collection of daylilies and immaculate vegetable patch; gardeners whose intricate, full-sleeve tattoos look more at home at a biker bar than they do plunged deep into a bag of potting soil; gardeners who haul wheelbarrows of mulch up steep hills well into their eighties; and gardeners who say goodbye to their beloved patch of marigolds on their first day of kindergarten. Gardening can strike anyone, at any age, at any time.

Much like diabetes, gardening can be Type 1 – developing in childhood – or Type 2, when a seemingly normal adult begins to exhibit adult-onset gardening. Though this is a topic of ongoing medical research, it is generally accepted that Type 1 gardening is inevitable and unpreventable, while Type 2 is triggered by dangerous lifestyle choices, such as spending time outside, enjoying beauty, and appreciating fresh, delicious food. People who go on to develop a bad case of gardening often obtain their first illicit taste from a family member or friend, although sometimes they are sucked into gardening by TV shows that make gardening look sexy and fun. Recognition of this danger has led the entertainment industry to severely restrict the amount of gardening content shown on television. Even channels like HGTV in the US, which ostensibly is about "Home and Garden," no longer carries dangerous gardening content – much as Coca-Cola long ago removed the cocaine from its popular beverage formulation. Sadly, however, a few tiny pockets of gardening remain on television, often airing at hours when impressionable children are watching. It is shocking that this state of affairs has been allowed to continue, given how gardening has been demonstrated numerous times to be far more addictive than softer but more restricted drugs, like crystal meth and heroin.

WARNING:
The following program protrays
gardens and **gardening**
PARENTAL DISCRETION IS ADVISED
Gardening is a serious condition.
Don't put your kids at risk.

Though some research suggests that adult-onset gardening can be prevented if proper steps are taken to inhibit exposure to nature, plants, and food that hasn't been highly processed and/or deep-fried, there is wide consensus that once full-blown gardening has developed, the condition is untreatable. Once a gardener, a gardener for life. You may have heard of the widely reported case of John Grant who was supposedly cured of gardening by a brutal regimen of electroshock therapy, but the researchers behind the purported cure were forced to retract their findings and resign in disgrace once it was discovered that although outside Mr. Grant's house there was nothing but lawn and a few boring shrubs, in his basement he had hidden away rack upon rack of grow lights over one of the most extensive collections of African violets and *Streptocarpus* in the world. The "cure" had, in fact, triggered a pattern of more extreme gardening.

So don't cling to some false hope that it is "just a phase," or that some new miracle cure will bring back the normal person you knew before; however, do not despair. Just because your gardener will never again pass a nursery without stopping to "just look around," and emerge an hour later with at least half a dozen plants in hand, does not mean that you must permit the gardener in your life to drive you bankrupt with endless plant shopping, or suffer as they fill your house with tender perennials they're intent on over-wintering every year. These and many other problematic behaviors can, with proper care and understanding, be managed so that you and your gardener may achieve a life that, at times, approaches the appearance of normalcy.

I write this book from a place of deep understanding. I, myself, suffer from congenital gardening. Though neither of my parents gardened, gardening runs in both of their families, and by the age of five I exhibited all the symptoms of full-blown gardening. I requested seeds for my birthday. I learned the name of every plant growing around our house. When, at age eight, I was told by my parents that we would be moving to a state nearly four hundred miles away, I lay in bed and cried—not over losing friends, but because I would leave behind the willow tree I had grown and nurtured from a cutting. If that sounds ridiculous, remember I was young. I would never do something like that now. As a mature adult I don't cry over willows. It would take losing a really nice tree, like a *Stewartia* or possibly a mature lacebark pine, to make me break down in tears these days.

Though stricken with such severe gardening at such a young age, I've learned to live a stable life and can sometimes even pass as relatively normal in casual social settings. I also know many gardeners, of all ages, and have observed their behaviors, both destructive and otherwise. This book is the product of all this experience, your guide to understanding the various behaviors and urges of the manic gardener in your life. I'll be giving you tips on how to keep gardeners healthy and happy, and information on how to prevent and treat some of the worst aspects of gardening behavior.

Through it all – even when loving a gardener feels overwhelming – remember that you are not alone, that many others suffer right along with you, and always keep in mind that it could be worse. Some people, after all, discover that the person they love is a gambler, a drug addict, or, worst of all, a golfer or football fan. At least with a gardener you get some tomatoes out of the deal.

Notable Behaviors of a Gardener

The habits of a gardener can be confusing, bizarre, and sometimes destructive. Recognizing these behaviors will help you cope with them from a place of sympathy, rather than simply being bewildered by the insanity. In this section, we'll go through some of the most mysterious and peculiar behaviors of gardeners and help you decide which behaviors you can try to manage and which you just need to accept. Please be warned, however, that there is no point in trying to comprehend the minds of the plant-obsessed. It is a simple truth that gardeners' brains don't work the same way as yours, and you must resign yourself to the fact that you are powerless to comprehend a true gardener's obsession with all that photosynthesizes.

Hating cute furry animals

You, as a normal person, likely find rabbits cute. You might even put food out—on purpose!—for squirrels and chipmunks. If you see a deer, you might reach for your camera to capture their beauty. A gardener sees things differently. They've spent hours and hours planting tulip bulbs only to turn around and see a squirrel following behind them, gobbling up each and every one. They know that rabbits have a voracious appetite for everything in the vegetable garden and, even worse, breed like, well, rabbits. You think the movie Bambi is sad because Bambi's mom dies. A gardener interprets it as sad because Bambi survives and will, no doubt, go on to jump a fence and mow down an entire garden full of prized roses and lilies. The only furry mammals a gardener loves are coyotes, wolves, and cats, because they eat those foul little rabbits, voles, and squirrels that rise up from hell to ruin everything that is good and photosynthetic.

    With this in mind, there are some ground rules when it comes to "cute" animals if you want to coexist peaceably with your gardener. First, don't feed the animals. And don't pretend that if you give them lots of food, they'll be so full they won't bother the garden. That's not how it works. Squirrels and rabbits and deer with lots of food show their gratitude by multiplying, by having lots of nasty little babies that then go on to destroy the garden. It is also well documented that deer in particular have an intense attraction to plants that are difficult to grow and will turn their noses up at the most appealing peanut butter treat in favor of destroying a particularly expensive or beloved specimen. Second, don't sympathize with the wretched monsters. If your gardener produces a device that delivers an electric shock to a squirrel, do NOT say, "Oh, poor little guy!" Keep that to yourself. Instead, cackle with feigned glee and say, "The little demon had it coming!" And, finally, cool it with the word "cute." No one wants to hear it. When a gardener stares down the face of evil itself while it sits in a tree, munching on a particularly choice cyclamen, the last thing they want to hear is the word "cute." Pestilence, plague, and destruction aren't cute. There is nothing cute about it. When it comes to squirrels, rabbits, deer, and the like, there is a simple rule: If you can't offer to stand watch night and day to chase them out of the garden, don't say anything at all.

Going nuts about stuff you can't see

From the depths of their plant obsession, your gardener sees the world very differently than you. Their vision is skewed and distorted in various bizarre, inexplicable ways. If they run into the living room holding a pot of dirt and yelling "It finally germinated!!!" your response should be to nod and pretend that you can see the tiny green speck they are waving about. It helps to say, "Wow, it did! Oh my God, I can't believe you finally got it to sprout! You are amazing!"

If they drag you to a nursery, spend forty minutes perusing a row of identical hostas that someone has jokingly labeled with all different names before they pull one out that looks just like all the rest and say to you, "Oh my God, LOOK AT THIS VARIETY!" the proper response is, "Wow. I… just… WOW."

Normal people see:

Gardeners see:

If, on the other hand, they hold up a perfectly normal looking basil leaf and say, tearfully, "Oh no! Downy mildew!" you should pretend to catch your breath and reply, "What?

Really? That's terrible!"

In short, gardeners will always be going on about something you can't see, don't understand, and simply don't give a crap about. The secret is not to let them know that you have no idea what they're babbling on about. It is easier than you might think. Just take your cue from your gardener and mirror their emotions. If they are happy, rejoice. If they sob, express your regret and pat their shoulder. For bonus points, follow up by asking a question. For example, if the news is good, ask how long they've been trying to get that particular plant to do whatever good thing they're rejoicing over, and the whole story will come pouring out. For any bad news, ask, "Did it happen last year?" This will prompt a long discussion of every variable of weather, garden arrangement, and variety selection that might have made this year different from or similar to every other growing season of the past decade. Once they get going, don't worry about listening, as there is no need. When they pause, throw in a "Really?" or "Uh huh?" and that's all they'll need from you to keep going. You can meanwhile focus your attention elsewhere, while they have a therapeutic talk, feeling like you really care.

Nursery crawling

Don't mistake this for merely shopping for plants. Nursery crawling is a complex behavior in its own right, a day-long affair usually performed with a group of gardening friends. The gardener goes from nursery to nursery studying plants, chatting up the staff about the newest varieties and spending hours browsing and comparing and Googling unfamiliar varieties on their smartphone before finally picking out choice treasures to bring home.

The purpose of a nursery crawl is not merely to acquire new plants (although that is certainly part of it because—let's be honest—acquiring new plants is part of nearly everything a gardener does). Nursery crawling is a social experience, a chance to bond and explore and chat. If your gardener regularly goes on nursery crawls alone, that's not good, and could be a sign that you must intervene for the sake of their health. You might be tempted to accompany them yourself—don't! The presence of a non-gardener will merely cramp their style, as non-gardeners all too often ask irrelevant questions like "How much does that cost?" and "But where are you going to plant it?"

Instead, try to arrange a nursery crawl play date with other gardeners. Many gardeners—undoubtedly including yours—are introverts, so you might need to take the initiative to make the nursery crawl happen. That is easily enough done. Just accompany them to a garden club meeting, hack into their Facebook account, or just walk up the street to any house with lots of plants and invite these other gardeners to go out for a nursery crawl. Going as a group will do wonders for your gardener's mental health, as shopping for plants is all the better when there is someone to ooh and aah with over a terrific begonia. And don't be afraid to invite that opinionated, cantankerous person from the garden club. Sometimes it is even more fun to fight over whether a plant is worth growing than agree they are all fabulous.

Whatever you do, when sending your gardener out on a nursery crawl, don't make the mistake of letting them take the minivan or SUV. Arrange with the other caregivers of gardeners in the group ahead of time to ensure all large vehicles will be unavailable that day, and send them off in the smallest possible compact car. The obvious benefit to you is that having limited cargo space will stop them maxing out quite as many credit cards.

But aside from that selfish reason, it will also prove more fun and challenging for your gardener. Half the nursery crawl experience is trying to pack too many plants into too small a car, and then driving home with one or more plants in your lap. A big vehicle with lots of space makes it too easy and spoils the fun.

Though social nursery crawling is a good, healthy bonding activity for your gardener, you should try to limit the frequency with which they take these trips. Make it a special treat, just once or twice a year, not unlike a holiday or birthday. Besides the obvious budgetary concerns, excessive nursery-hopping only serves to increase your gardener's chances of getting pot-constipated.

Pot constipation

You may not know pot constipation by that name, but anyone who has spent time with a gardener knows what it looks like and how it develops. Your gardener goes to the nursery and comes back with a carload of plants in pots. The pots get unloaded along the side of the house and the gardener assures you that they'll get them in the ground on their next free afternoon. After all, there's no more free time today because they've blown the entire day at the nursery.

Come the next sunny, open day, they do plant a few – but only a few – and the rest linger, the pots full of plants sitting there waiting. The next available day, your gardener makes another nursery trip because there is a sale simply too irresistible to pass up, and then yet another trip, "just because…" More and more pots build up, but none of them are moving on to the actual garden. As the pot constipation grows in severity, plants may start dying because they're not getting properly watered. It becomes impossible to park your car in the driveway, and the mail can't be delivered because no one can make it to the front door without tripping over an enormous *Miscanthus*.

The primary cause of pot constipation is over-thinking—or, more accurately, under-thinking followed by over-thinking. Under-thinking is when the gardener grabs a bunch of cool-looking plants at the nursery with no plan, no room for them, and no thought whatsoever. They simply buy up everything with a striking flower or leaf. Though you can try and prevent this under-thinking by encouraging your gardener to draw up plans and shopping lists, don't kid yourself. Even the best-laid plans are quickly upended by a display of incredible Siberian irises in full bloom.

Once the impulse purchase arrives home, the gardener begins to over-think, surveying the garden for the ideal spot for their new plants and worrying that they will clash with the roses over here or be too tall for the *Campanula* over there. After walking around the garden for an hour – second-guessing every possible location – they give up, mentally exhausted, and head out to the nursery because shopping for plants, they claim, helps to sow the seeds for inspiration.

The solution? What is dubbed by the wonderful Carol Michel, creator of the "May Dreams Gardens" blog, as a "Plopper's Field." Or, if you must be snooty about it, a nursery bed. Whatever you call it, it's a spot in the garden where your gardener can just evacuate everything in a pot that they don't know what to do with. Plopped into the ground, plants are far easier to care for, and the gardener can take their sweet time to look around, observe each plant through the seasons, the move each iris and geranium to a more permanent location once the gardener knows where each will look best.

Though a good plopper's field can do a lot to alleviate pot constipation, be warned that gardeners risk developing secondary pot constipation: the mindless hoarding of countless empty nursery pots. You can try reasoning with them that surely a dozen or so spare pots is all they could possibly need, that if they find they really need three thousand pots at some point, they can easily borrow them from their like minded gardening friends. But don't expect it to work. The empty pots will continue to build up, clogging first the shed and then the garage. Once they populate in high enough numbers, empty nursery pots have been shown to breed and reproduce at ever-increasing rates until they spill out into the street and block traffic.

Ignore protests that these provide a welcome community service because they slow down traffic to safer levels. Telling your gardener to do something with all those pots is useless. They'll just continue to assert how they will eventually need them all for some obscure reason. No, you must take action. Tell your gardener that you have found somewhere to recycle used nursery pots. (If you can find a place to do so, that's great; otherwise, assure them you have and then load up every pot you can find and chuck them in the garbage.) The key to eliminating pot constipation is regularity, so be prepared to repeat the process annually to keep the pot population below the threshold where they can start reproducing.

Showing off on social media

These days, everyone seems to be addicted to Facebook, Twitter, and Instagram, but these social media sites hold a particularly special place in the gardener's heart. Gardening can be isolating. It is a solitary activity and all too often the "other" people a gardener knows in real life are more interested in dull, unimportant things like football or shoes or raising children.

What the plant looks like:

What you post online:

❤ 3,204

🗨 Wow!

🗨 Wish mine looked like that!

Organizations like garden clubs and plant societies go a long way to mitigate the isolation of a gardener, but sometimes the gentians go into dazzling, perfect, incredible peak bloom weeks away from any garden meeting or gathering and your gardener has to share them with someone. Someone who will really get it – that is, someone who won't just smile and say, "That's pretty."

Your gardener needs to upload that photo with a falsely casual caption like, "Some of my gentians are looking okay..." and then sit hunched over the computer waiting anxiously for comments like "OKAY??? Those are GORGEOUS!" and, most satisfying of all, "What's your secret? I've killed them more times than I can count!" At that point, your gardener smirks and feels brilliant as they type out smug replies like, "I don't really have a secret. I just plop them in the ground and they grow."

In addition to showing off, they can join all sorts of online gardening groups and forums where they can ask questions and get a bunch of other knowledgeable people to identify that plant they've been wondering about. Even better, your gardener can show off how smart they are by correcting someone else when they use the outdated *Aster* instead of the preferred *Symphyotrichum*.

As annoying as it may be, you can turn those times when your gardener is online, chatting away with other gardeners, into useful opportunities. If you're out while your gardener is home mucking about with their plants, get out your smartphone before you return and see what photos they've shared and what people are saying about them. Then, when you arrive, casually walk around the garden and exclaim, "My God, those gentians are amazing! I cannot believe how beautiful they are! Aren't they supposed to be hard to grow?" Your gardener will swell with pride and feel like you really care. They never need to know that you haven't the faintest idea what a gentian looks like, and that you are simply repeating what you read in the comments on their photos.

Apologizing for weeds that aren't there

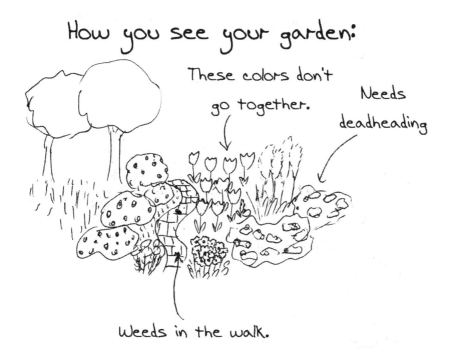

It happens every time someone comes to visit the garden. Your gardener, instead of showing off the lovely flowers or gorgeous tomatoes, spends the entire time apologizing for everything being a weedy mess and saying that such and such had looked good last week but is a total disaster now and they're so embarrassed for anyone to see it. They'll say this even if just yesterday they dragged you into the garden, bursting with pride, to show you the first bloom on their new camellia. As soon as a visitor shows up, they don't point out the beautiful bloom but instead apologize that there are so few of them.

How visitors see your garden:

I wish I could grow those!

Lovely!

Love the stone work!

This strange behavior is nearly universal to gardeners and is the result of a particular form of location-specific vision known as "gardener's myopia." When they are in their home territory, gardeners only see problems and the things that need to be done. Every weed, every ragged edge, every uncut blade of grass they see with perfect clarity, but the lovely flowers, the harmonious

26

colors, the lush vegetable garden are all blurry, out of focus. When the gardener leaves their own garden and visits another, their vision switches and they see with crystal clarity the fragrant phlox and abundant peppers, oblivious to the occasional weed or mildewed leaf.

When gardener's myopia is overcome, it leads to improved quality of life as the gardener can now enjoy the beauty they have created. They experience the pleasure of inviting gardening friends over without obsessing that everything has to be absolutely perfect, and they are now inspired by the gardens they visit without being overwhelmed by feelings of inadequacy. Sadly, curing gardener's myopia is difficult if not impossible, but sometimes your ability to recognize the symptoms and the condition can help a gardener adjust their vision to where they can enjoy their own garden more.

Running out of space

In college, your gardener filled the windowsill and tiny balcony of your apartment to overflowing with plants. Out of necessity, you bought a house with a nice little space in which to garden and in seemingly no time, it began to burst at the seams. Then, the nice older lady next door said your gardener could use some of her space, and, BAM! – they suddenly need that collection of old roses they've been dreaming about. Inspired (and feeling exceedingly pleased with yourself), you set out to secure them a spot in the community garden or allotment. Intoxicated, they decide they must grow thirty different kinds of tomatoes to see which ones they like the best. To make them happy, you move out of the city to a country house boasting several acres and, well, you know what happens next. It is not a destination—it is an endless treadmill. When you grow weary of them fretting about running out of space for new vegetable beds and perennial borders, you find yourself tempted to move to a two-hundred-acre farm. Wait! Know that as soon as you do, they will lack sufficient space for their orchard, arboretum, and re-creation of a Provence lavender field.

The most common nightmare of normal people living next to gardeners

Running out of room for plants is what gardeners do. It is a fundamental part of their nature, as instinctive and fundamental as a beaver building a dam or a deer decimating a prized collection of lilies.

The secret is to avoid giving gardeners a lot of space at once. If you live in an urban area, sending them to beg for space from neighbors or to apply to the local government to turn a vacant lot into a garden, will give them new spaces in dribs and drabs and keep the explosive garden growth under control. If you intend to move to some wonderful acreage in the country, you can always resort to subterfuge to slow the inevitable garden expansion. Simply bribe a surveyor to pretend that your property line is much shallower, and that the meadow beyond belongs to some obscure, absentee owner. Then, after a few years, when they're itching for more room, either discover the "mistake" or, even better, "buy" them the rest of your property for their birthday! They'll be beside themselves with joy and you will forestall the inevitable complaining about not having enough space for another few years.

Zonal denial

The U.S. Department of Agriculture has divided the country into horticultural zones based on average winter low temperatures. These zones are intended as a guide to help gardeners understand what plants will thrive in their local conditions, particularly in terms of surviving the winter, and which are destined to perish. The problem is that gardeners interpret these zones not as a guideline but a challenge, and as soon as they are told they can't grow a plant in their zone, they are determined to try to grow it anyway.

So, if you live in what the USDA classifies as zone 5, your gardener will constantly try to grow plants that are only winter hardy to the warmer zones 6 and 7, and each and every spring you will find them either elated that their "hardy" banana survived, or weeping over dead, mushy remains. Move south to zone 7 and, rather than reveling in all the plants that would have frozen in their old garden, they insist on trying to grow plants better suited to zones 8 or 9. Head all the way south to some balmy, subtropical, frost-free clime and, without fail, gardeners go in the opposite direction, piling mounds of ice over their peonies or digging up daffodil bulbs and storing them in the refrigerator crisper drawer for several months,to fool the plants into thinking they've weathered winter and to bloom, while shrugging dismissively at palm trees and orchids.

Now, you might say (as did the USDA), "Wouldn't it make more sense if instead of denying their climatic conditions, the gardener embraced them? If they focused on finding and enjoying all the amazing plants that will thrive in their location without any special care?" The answer is yes, of course that would be the best option, were gardeners rational beings. The problem is, they aren't. They are capricious and ridiculous, and constantly lust after the things they can't grow instead of enjoying what they can. There is no cure for this nonsensical zonal denial. You just have to accept it.

Being part of one big gossipy gardening family

Perhaps you, as a normal person, have a hobby. Maybe you like photography or knitting or golf. You might be tempted to think of gardening as just another hobby. It is not. Gardening is a lifestyle, an identity. It is even a community. If you were to meet someone at a party who shares your interest, you might chat with them about it, but that's about the extent of the connection. A gardener, on the other hand, will invite another gardener they have never met before to stay at your house.

This may seem like an exaggeration. It isn't. I have, multiple times, stayed at the homes of people I'd never met before, been offered dinner, rides, advice, and free plants by total strangers, and had people invite not just me but my parents to parties sight unseen, simply because I'm a gardener and they're a gardener, and so, therefore, that makes us family.

Now, there are many wonderful things about being part of the gardening family. But you should know that, like so many families, it is a gossipy one. I once met a man for the first time at a gardening conference where I was speaking, and as I shook his hand and said, "So nice to meet you!" I was thinking about all the rumors I'd heard about his new wife—how so-and-so thought they hadn't dated long enough before getting married, how someone else thought she was weird and standoffish, while yet a third person was reserving judgment but thought she seemed nice enough. Gardeners like to gossip.

So, when you share your life with a gardener, be prepared. When you travel, know that your gardener is sure to be e-mailing and telephoning and securing invitations to see gardens and have dinner and stay with people they've never met face to face. Don't be surprised when your gardener casually mentions one day that a stranger is going to be staying a couple of days in the guest room. Ask who this person is and they'll say, "Oh, he's got an amazing collection of irises and cyclamen, and the stone walls in his garden—just lovely." If you try to follow up with how your gardener knows this person, you are wasting your time, because you'll just get more facts about their garden. You have to accept that, to a gardener, the only proof they need that a person is a decent human being is that they are a serious gardener. And, the fact is, they are right. Gardeners are good people. They just are. Weird, bizarre, eccentric, yes, but good.

Now, the flip side of all this is that if you, as a non-gardener, marry a gardener, you can expect the gardening world to be suspicious. You have no cyclamen collection or crevice garden to recommend you. What makes you good enough to marry into the family? You'll have to win them over, which, luckily, is easy enough to do. Whenever you spend time with other gardeners, talk about nothing except how much you enjoy the garden, how impressed you are by everything your gardener does, and how you always do everything in your power to support and help them in their gardening endeavors. If you can't be a gardener, loving and admiring and supporting one is nearly good enough. With the gardening gossip network being what it is, you only have to say this once and word will spread faster than an invasive weed to the whole horticultural family that you might just be worthy of one of their own.

Looking forward

Actors and models look backwards, mourning their fading youth and beauty. Athletes peak in their twenties, and spend the rest of their life remembering how they were once great. Gardeners, on the other hand, look forward. Each year yields more blooms from the steadily increasing crocuses, a new generation in a breeding project, and broader branches on the beloved tree that was only a little whip when it was planted. No sooner has time closed the door on one growing season than the gardener is looking forward to what they will plant next year, wondering whether the *Davidia* will finally bloom, figuring out which new varieties of tomatoes to try, and scheming a new

34

perennial bed in the back.

Normal people and gardeners experience the passage of time differently.

Even as they age and slow down, gardeners look forward. Even when they have to reduce the size of the vegetable garden, the orchard keeps growing and producing, and when they don't have the energy to divide the perennials, the bark on the *Stewartia* continues to grow more beautiful. To garden is to anticipate. And that isn't a bad thing.

Being happy

Some studies suggest there are bacteria in the soil that act as anti-depressants. Maybe it is something about getting enough vitamin D by being out in the sun, or simply the pleasure of working hard to create beautiful flowers and delicious food. Whatever the reason, gardeners are happy people. This is worth remembering when you stare at the credit card bill in horror and see how much your gardener spent on mulch, or trip over the huge pots of tender perennials they hope to overwinter in the one sunny window. As frustrating as living with someone with a plant addiction can be, there are worse things than having them spend their time doing something that fills them with joy.

Seasons of the Gardener

Normal people often misinterpret gardeners as moody, going from quiet and depressed to wildly manic and busy, before slowly mellowing out again. But, far from being unpredictable or the symptom of some mental disorder (other than, of course, gardening), the changeable habits and behaviors of gardeners are entirely knowable once you understand one simple fact: gardeners are seasonal creatures. Just as the plants they love respond to changing temperature, day length, and rainfall by putting out leaves, flowering, and then going dormant, so too gardeners change with the seasons. A gardener in early summer may be almost unrecognizable as the person they were months before in the depth of winter.

Understanding these seasonal shifts in behavior is critical to properly understanding and caring for the gardener in your life. In this section, we discuss the typical seasonal behaviors, but every gardener is different and each responds in their own unique way to the changing seasons. Keep a gardener calendar, and note what times of year trigger plant shopping binges or precisely when in summer the damage done to their garden by animals drives them to throw shovels and shriek hysterically at passing squirrels. Mark the moment they go from reveling in the beauty of their fall crocuses to hunching over and whimpering at the thought of the impending arrival of winter. Noting these events will help you to plan ahead for the next year. And by planning, I mean planning a trip out of town so you don't have to deal with it.

Winter

Winter is the dormant season when the gardener hunkers down under a pile of warm blankets surrounded by the houseplants and enormous tropical plants they want to overwinter. Winter is, of course, the season gardeners love to hate, the season they complain about endlessly. Truth be told, however, there are a lot of important functions for winter in the life of a gardener. There are also a lot of annoyances and strange habits to be endured. Winter is the time when you, the normal person in your gardener's life, need to be on your toes, ready for all four phases of a gardener's passage through the winter season.

Phase one: rest

Gardening is a lot of work. Though there are gardeners who have adapted to climates like those of Southern California and are capable of gardening nonstop with no winter break for most gardeners winter is a critical period to escape the incessant weeding and watering and relax while the snow piles up and the garden slumbers. This is the good part of winter, and during the resting period you, as the keeper of a gardener, need to do little more than look for ways to enhance that rest, to make it even more restful. Warm blankets are critical, as is a constant supply of chocolate (both hot and in bar form) and it is a good time to distract the gardener with other hobbies. Perhaps they like to cook or knit or make taxidermy owls. Now is the time to remind them of these hobbies and allow them to spend a few months distracted, so they return to the garden fresh and energized come spring.

Ah winter...
when a young gardener's
fancy turns to...

Books.

Phase two: planning

During the frenzy of the growing season, gardeners are so busy weeding, watering, and harvesting that they don't have time to sit down and think about what is working, what isn't, and what they want to do next year. That is what winter is for, and once the rest period is over and your gardener is showing signs of restlessness, it is time to start to plan. There are lots of things you can do to encourage and facilitate good winter planning. Buy a new book on garden design or a gorgeous guide to unusual heirloom vegetables. Scroll through pictures of the garden taken at various points during the season and ask them what they think worked well and what didn't.

You may be tempted to make the planning process more efficient and effective. Don't. That would be a grave mistake. Instead, as soon as they've settled on a new formal garden full of square beds and clipped hedges, you should produce a bunch of books advocating casual, sweeping meadows and prairies. After they've spent the next week researching plants for a moonlight garden, suddenly remember that you are severely allergic to fragrant white flowers. Whatever you can do to obstruct, delay, and misdirect, do it. The goal of a successful winter planning season is to force the gardener to take their time. Don't let them rush through a plan and order a bajillion plants, all in one day. Besides the fact that long-pondered plans turn out better, if they rush through the planning process too fast, they are liable to get bored over the course of the rest of the winter, and boredom during the winter can lead to various disordered behaviors, including, but not limited to, manic late-night plant shopping binges. Drag it out. More planning, more better.

Phase three: cabin fever

As winter drags on and planning is completed, cabin fever sets in and your gardener begins to get anxious. They often develop nervous tics, perhaps pacing up and down in front of windows. Or they bundle up and go for walks through the snow-covered garden even though there is nothing to see or do there. If left untreated, cabin fever leads to binge shopping on a devastating scale and sowing tomatoes so early that they are root bound and leggy by the time spring planting season arrives. While the only real cure for cabin fever is the arrival of spring, there are stopgap measures you can implement.

If possible, get the gardener out of the house. A trip to a local conservatory filled with warm, humid air and lush, growing plants can be enormously beneficial, as can a vacation to a warmer locale. When your gardener is at home, throw any distraction at them you can think of. Get a fish tank or a new cookbook. Pretend to break your leg so they have to spend their day waiting on you. Propose marriage and force them to plan an elaborate ceremony and reception, or, if you are already married, threaten to divorce them or insist on marriage counseling. Anything—anything at all—to keep their mind off the endless expanse of snow and the long weeks of waiting ahead.

Phase Four: seed starting

The light at the end of the tunnel is when, finally—*finally* —it is time for your gardener to start sowing seeds for this year's tomatoes, peppers, and tender annuals. Now, you might imagine that having your basement or bedroom closet filled with lights while your gardener spills potting soil and seeds everywhere is the last thing you want, but, trust me, if your gardener has never started anything indoors from seed, you want to get them doing so, this and every winter. Once they have lights to fuss with, seed packets to pore over, dirt to endlessly scrutinize for the tiniest sign of movement, and then seedlings to observe and pots to water, they will stop griping about the endless winter. If you can get them to start their seeds early, I can almost guarantee you won't catch them up at 1 a.m. with the credit card, feverishly ordering an entire orchard of peach trees. Starting seeds indoors is the perfect late winter distraction. If your gardener has trouble generating healthy seedlings, consider buying them an extra set of lights to hang next to the ones they have, as more light makes for dramatically healthier, sturdier seedlings. A small fan to create a little air movement goes a long way toward preventing problems with damping off.

During all phases of the winter experience it is important to ensure your gardener gets plenty of exercise. If your gardener just sits around all winter, come spring, when they spend an entire Saturday digging holes, pruning trees, and hauling wheelbarrows full of mulch, they'll wind up spending the next day lying on the couch, moaning piteously over their sore muscles. This is, of course, incredibly annoying, as it is difficult to turn the TV volume up loud enough to drown out their moans.

To head this situation off, make sure your gardener stays active during the winter. The usual things (like a gym membership) can help, but sometimes the best thing is to sneak up behind them, jerk that seed catalog out of their hands, and throw it as far as you can outside into the snow. Think of it in the same terms as throwing a ball for a dog. Desperate to sift through the many options of tomatoes they want to grow next year, they'll sprint out to retrieve the catalog, at which point the frigid air will force them to sprint back equally as fast to the warmth of the house. Repeat every few hours and your gardener will come out of the winter in perfect shape, ready to garden their little heart out.

Forget Robins... the REAL first sign of spring is tomato seedlings!

Spring

The arrival of spring, in all its frenzied glory, is when you realize why gardeners need that winter rest. Spring is nothing short of manic. The snow starts to melt and your gardener begins to creep around the garden every day, inspecting every inch of ground for signs of emerging crocuses and daffodils, poking at

46

dormant perennials and scratching at the twigs of shrubs, wondering if they succumbed to that vicious cold snap back in January. Then, all at once, the ground has dried out enough to work and they rush here and there, cutting things back and planting peas and lettuce, moving perennials they chide themselves for foolishly having waited until now to move, while the FedEx man, UPS woman, and mail carrier all chat on the front porch as they pile up more and more boxes of plants, all ordered during the depths of the cabin fever phase last winter. Every box needs to be opened and examined. A flurry of activity ensues as the gardener has to figure out where on earth—literally!—they are going to put the twenty-five peach trees, small forest of tropical hibiscus, the two-dozen-plant sampler of hostas, and the sixteen kinds of potatoes, all of which they had totally forgotten they'd ordered and must now share the only open space in the garden, which is a grand total of four square feet.

During this frenzy, your gardener will to rejoice over the crocuses which have spread even more this year, despair over the squirrel-decimated tulips, take countless photos of everything to show their gardener friends, and spend hours chatting with other gardeners—in person and online—about what has come back and what hasn't, what looks its best this year, and whether that new lilac really lives up to all the hype.

Through all of this, your role in taking care of the gardener in the spring is mostly to make sure they eat. If you aren't careful, they'll work all night and then shove an entire of box of Oreos in their mouth before heading back out into the garden. Cook or buy them some nutritious food—and make sure it includes plenty of that critical food group, chocolate—and put it out in the garden where they can't miss it. Chances are, if they have to move a plate of food to get to the wheelbarrow, they'll eat the food while doing so. Other than that, simply accept that your gardener will not be around, so, yes, you are going to have to go to that party by yourself and keep out of their way. Spring is crazy, and a bit lonely for people who love a gardener, but it is brief and the calmer days of summer will be here before you know it.

The more is snows the more I shops.

Summer

Summer is the season of dreams fulfilled, when all the anticipation and planning of winter and the frenzied work of spring bears literal as well as figurative fruit in the garden. The long-coddled vegetable seedlings grow and begin to produce the most delicious tomatoes you've ever tasted, the carefully planted rows of gladioli send up their spikes of vivid color, and the dreams of winter are realized more beautifully, richly, and flavorfully than your gardener could have ever imagined.

Except, of course, when they aren't—when there is a drought, or a herd of deer moves in, or a plague of slugs appears of out thin air, or a mysterious blight kills an entire crop of lovingly tended basil plants.

Every gardener's summer has the good, the bad, and, yes, even the ugly. To take care of your gardener, help them to appreciate the good, mourn alongside them over the bad, and distract them from the ugly. Do this by enjoying—effusively—the armfuls of flowers and vegetables they bring into the house— drool and enthuse over each and every one, even if you privately think there are nicer ones available at the grocery store. Take a long walk through the garden now and again single out plants and exclaim how beautiful they are. Inhale deeply the fragrance of every rose, and thank your gardener for creating such a wonderland.

When disaster strikes, sit with your gardener, ask them

sympathetically what happened, curse the evil mammals or fungi or insects or misleading catalog descriptions that caused the problem, and then, after a few minutes, ask them a question about the prettiest, most flower- or vegetable-laden plant you can see. Ask what it is, why it grows so beautifully, and in no time at all your gardener will be sufficiently distracted from their tragedy to enthusiastically tell you far more than anyone ever wanted to know about the proper culture of bearded irises.

Summer is also the season of unexpected chores. The frenzy of spring is—or should be—proactive, carefully planned (if it isn't, God help you and your gardener), with the last frost date marked on the calendar and careful drawings of each bed showing that the tomatoes go here and the petunias there. Summer, on the other hand, is reactive, the season when you must deal with what the weather throws at you, and that unexpectedness means you need to be ready to pitch in, as needed. A long, hot, dry spell will require you to drag hoses and water for long hours, while a blustery storm blowing in will send you and the gardener rushing out to stake those dahlias before they wind up smashed in the mud.

Along with all this, be sure to take lots of photos of the garden through the whole growing season, with multiple angles of every section and bed. Gardeners always, always document a thousand times the first crocus or daffodil to bloom, but, come summer, they forget, and months go by without them having snapped a single picture. Imagine their delight and gratitude when you do it for them, as having an exhaustive photo catalog of what the garden looked like this year will prove enormously helpful when you need to prolong the planning stage next winter. After all, they will have to pore through each and every photo, many of which they won't have seen before, and analyze what is working, what isn't, and what they'll do differently next year. It is never too early to think about what you can do to get your gardener to weather the coming winter!

But, mostly—and don't forget this, and don't let your gardener forget this—summer is the season to enjoy. Pour a couple of glasses of wine, open a box of chocolates, and take a moment to sit outside and enjoy a long summer evening, gazing out over the garden and all its boisterous, exuberant summer bounty.

Autumn

As summer slips away, leaves begin to flush red and orange and gold, a chill arrives in the evening air, and the warm busyness of summer slips into the quiet, meditative calm of fall.

Fall is arguably the easiest season in which to live with a gardener. As it winds down, the number of chores to be done drops off, and the anxieties of summer, over too much or too little rain, or the most recent pest plague, fade from the urgent present to vague memories of the past. There is still planting to be done, naturally, but compared to the frenzy of spring planting, fall is far more relaxed. Most of the work is putting in bulbs, which require little fuss, have no roots or stems to break, and won't dry out if they don't get in the ground soon enough. There are only long, blissful afternoons spent in the crisp fall air, plunging little brown lumps into the ground and imagining the glorious sweeps of color they are destined to become when spring returns.

Fall in the garden has become even less work these days as more and more gardeners forgo the traditional fall cleanup (cutting back of perennials and sweeping away every errant leaf) in favor of leaving perennials to stand over the winter to look wild and natural, with snow on their seed heads, while various insects —hopefully mostly beneficial or striking ones—overwinter in their leafy bases. This undeniably makes for more work in the spring, but that is what spring is for. If the gardener didn't have myriad chores in the spring, they wouldn't know what to do with all their pent-up energy. So, by all means encourage your gardener to leave everything as it is, telling them it is better for the local ecosystem (whether true or not) if they relax as much as possible in the autumn.

Those peaceful days of fading glory, however, will be rudely interrupted the day your gardener hears the word "frost" or, worse, "freeze" in the weather report. At that moment, they can be seen sprinting out to the garden to madly haul containers of tropical plants into the house, digging up enormous tender perennials that they pledged, when planted, that they would treat as annuals and let die at season's end, but, oh my goodness, just look how pretty they are! Why not try to save them, or at least a few? It is such a shame to abandon them all to freeze to death. Why pay to acquire more down the road when you have these here right now that are in perfectly good condition? All at once, your living room, which was lovely, with its vase brimming with late dahlias and a bowl of colorful gourds, has been transformed into a giant jungle of sprawling plants spilling leaves, trailing dirt, and dribbling water everywhere while the cat goes nuts trying to smell, investigate, nibble, climb, and knock over each new addition. You will desperately want to scream and start hurling the enormous vegetative excess into the trash. I urge you, however, to breathe and think this through.

The battle over bringing plants indoors for the winter is a serious one for anyone who lives with a gardener. On the one hand, it's true that the more plants they overwinter, the less they'll (hopefully) insist on buying next spring, so there is a money saving side to all of this. Plus, overwintering house plants and tender perennials goes a long way toward relieving winter stress in the gardener, as it gives them something green and growing to look at and fuss over during those interminably long cold months. On the other hand, it gets old fast, not being able to walk through the living room without a machete, and having your wood floors warped and ruined by errant watering cans. The solution? It is all a matter of finding the right balance.

When it comes to over wintering plants indoors...

Honey could you hold this ONE pot on your lap? Just until spring?

...it is possible to go too far.

There are a couple strategies to dealing with the influx of

tender plants all winter. First, many plants can be forced into dormancy by simply keeping them cool and dry. Shove tropical hibiscus, almost all begonias, *Brugmansia*, and *Pelargonium* away in a dark corner of the basement or a spare room, stop watering them, and they'll drop their leaves and sit there, dormant and inert, requiring no care or even light. Come spring, add water, move them outside, and they'll come back to life almost miraculously, without ever having turned your living room into Little Shop of Horrors. The same goes for almost all succulent plants, and is worth trying with other tropical plants that your gardener doesn't have room for under lights or in a sunny window. Letting these plants go dormant out of sight in the basement is a perfect compromise. You save money while they save plants, and you limit the nuisance factor by evicting them from high-traffic living areas.

The other strategy is to choose the right tropical plants and annuals for the garden in the first place. Many plants traditionally featured as houseplants transition to terrific annuals outside in the summer, and then back indoors, smoothly and attractively, rather than turning into that leggy, awful mess you are forced to stare at and step around all winter. Instead of impatiens in that shady border, suggest African violets or their gorgeous relatives, *Streptocarpus*. Classic houseplant bromeliads provide dramatic accents in a summer container and move inside looking equally good on a winter windowsill. These plants will make your house look gorgeous and flowery all winter, instead of some kind of torture camp for plants that would prefer to be off in Florida somewhere.

Once the plants have all moved into their various winter locations, the garden has been put to bed, and all bulbs planted, take your gardener off for some long walks through local woods to enjoy the fading autumn sunshine through lingering leaves, and the brisk autumnal air. Have them soak up all the outside time they can, while you mentally brace for the task of getting them through the coming winter.

Care and Feeding of Gardeners

For all their peculiarities, gardeners are generally easy to care for, requiring less fuss, in fact, than the majority of normal people. Most of the time all that is needed is to simply keep out of their way and let them garden. But no human is totally pest- and problem-free. Even the most independent gardener needs a little TLC now and then. As always, consult your doctor and local nursery before making any decision about the health of your gardener.

Weathering the weather

Every year, without fail, your gardener will get distressed about the weather. It may be a late frost, an early thaw, drought, rain that just won't stop, a summer so hot the lettuce all bolts overnight, or one so cold the tomatoes never ripen. Don't for a second think that most years are "normal" to the gardener. The latest research shows that there are, on average, 6.5 shockingly horrifying weather events per gardener per year. In fact, a year without unusual weather is not normal; it is one for the record books and should be cause for celebration, although, in all likelihood, your gardener will be too busy dealing with an unprecedented outbreak of grasshoppers, Japanese beetles, or the worst rabbit damage in living memory to notice the abnormally normal weather.

Normal Person:

Gardener:

When that crazy, unheard of bad weather does arrive, your first course of action should be to ask how you can help. If an unexpected frost is headed your way, grab all the bed sheets, including those on your bed, and spread them over the garden as directed by your panicking gardener. Before you protest, let me remind you that even the nicest, most expensive, high-thread-count sheets can be washed. And you're not gonna die if you don't have sheets to sleep between for one night, so stop acting like you need them for the bed. Learn to share. And then, in the aftermath of this alarming spate of weather, once you have done whatever you can, your next task is to help with the mourning process.

When terrible weather happens, there is always a way to put a positive spin on it. The worst possible summer for tomatoes and peppers is invariably the best possible summer for lettuce and peas, and even in the longest drought there will be plants that surprise you by thriving despite the dryness, and blooming better than they have in years. In a bad weather crisis, your instinct will naturally be to point out these silver linings. "It isn't so bad," you'll be tempted to say. "Look on the bright side!" Don't. Don't do it. Trust me. You may have the best intentions in the world, your little pep talks might even have validity, but in their moment of weather tragedy, your gardener needs time to mourn, not listen to you babble some inane positive thinking. Yes, the fact that the old maple tree blew down in the storm will indeed let in the very light they've been hankering after to grow some fabulous lilies. That is true. But would you put a hand on the shoulder of someone mourning the loss of a beloved grandmother and suggest they cheer up because they now stand to inherit a bunch of money? Because that's just what it's going to sound like! Please, don't do it. When weather strikes, take your gardener's hand, wrap it around some chocolate, and say, "I'm so sorry. That really sucks." Then, keep handing them chocolate and repeating that as long as they need you to. When they're ready to move on, you'll know, because they'll reach for a catalog and start to shop for those lilies to sink into that new sunny spot in the garden.

The sun

Gardeners are rarely deficient in vitamin D, but all those hours outside make them frequent victims of brutal sunburns. It is up to you to make sure your gardener is protected. Buy them several wide-brimmed hats and keep multiple bottles of sunscreen scattered around—put some by the back door and in the shed by the trowel. Hang a bottle of sunscreen and a hat by a string from the rose arbor so it will smack them in the face and remind them not to burn to a crisp. But don't expect that to work. Sure, if your gardener is planning to spend an afternoon in the garden, they might put on the hat and sunscreen, but the problem is, gardeners mostly don't *plan* to spend long periods in the garden. They go out for two seconds to see whether the beans have germinated, spy some weeds behind the hedge, and before they know it, three hours have passed and the back of their neck is glowing the same shade of red as the handles of their Felco pruners. You simply can't rely on gardeners to remember other, less important things once they get gardening, so you, the normal person, will have to take action. Every time they say they're just going out in the garden for a second, check on them a couple of minutes later. If they're bent over, pulling weeds, staking dahlias, or harvesting tomatoes, grab the biggest container of sunscreen you can and squirt, aiming for any exposed skin. Chances are they'll be so busy trying to wiggle the entire taproot of a dandelion out of the ground without breaking it that they won't even notice, so just hose them down with sunscreen and rub it in. Then, set a timer for yourself and head out again every hour or two, squeeze bottle in hand, to apply a new layer to replace the earlier one that's been washed away with sweat. And when you do, bring along a tall glass of cold water or iced tea to keep your gardener hydrated. Yes, they should grasp that just as they have to water the plants, they need to water themselves. But that would mean they would be thinking like a normal person. They don't. Gardeners forget themselves when they garden and are swept away into the world of burgeoning plants and bright flowers. That's kind of the point, and, frankly, to the gardener, a little sunburn or heat exhaustion now and again is totally worth it.

Helping in the garden

You may find yourself looking out the window on occasion, at a garden in full bloom, while eating a dinner made entirely of fresh, impossibly delicious, home-grown produce, a vase of elegant flowers gracing the dining table before you, and you think, "This gardening thing is wonderful! My gardener works so hard. I wish I could help out somehow." Most of the time, this feeling vanishes moments later, when you open this month's credit card statement to find a $5,000 purchase at the local nursery they'd hoped you wouldn't notice, or come into the kitchen to find the countertop buried beneath cups of tomato slime, fermenting and molding in some bizarre seed extraction procedure, or notice that your beloved gardener has tracked muddy footprints all over the floor you just mopped. At that moment, you find yourself wishing you lived with a more normal human. Nonetheless, if you are feeling extraordinarily charitable, and your gardener is exceptionally nice and respectful, you may still want to help out.

The problem is that when non-gardeners try to help out in the garden they often inadvertently cause more harm than good. Here are some tips to ensure you don't ruin your gardener's day when all you wanted to do was something nice:

1. Be *sure* it is a weed. Yes, it looks like a weed. You may be one hundred percent certain that it's a dandelion. You might even be right. That said, your gardener may have also spent an absurd amount of money ordering pink dandelion seeds from England, only three of which germinated. So, be aware that if you pull it out, it could result in heartbreak. (This is all entirely hypothetical. When I ordered pink dandelion seeds from another country, I had four germinate.) All those little seedlings you just pulled because they weren't planted in neat lines like everything else in the garden and look just like Queen Anne's lace, could have been your gardener's favorite self-sowing annual *Nigella*. So

be sure before you pull. Your gardener, of course, would never make this mistake because they know all the plants in the garden. For you, on the other hand, trying to learn the entire catalog of desirable plants living in the garden may be on par with memorizing the American Horticultural Society's *Encyclopedia of Garden Plants*. Your best course of action is to ask your gardener to show you their most despised weed, just one specific plant you can learn to reliably identify. Be sure you can tell it from the other plants in the garden and then go nuts on that particular weed. Sure, you will miss some other equally noxious weeds, but let me tell you, when your gardener discovers that their *Oxalis* plague has finally been brought under control, they'll love you forever.

2. Do it their way. I observed the importance of this when I lived next door to a charming couple. She loved to garden. He loved power tools. Saturday afternoons often were punctuated by an engine roaring to life, followed by the shriek, "NO NO! NOT THERE!" That tiller may seem like an efficient way to rid the garden of all those weeds—until, that is, you see your gardener on their knees, weeping over the shredded remains of a few thousand dormant crocus bulbs you didn't know about. Trust me, just do it their way. If they hand you a narrow shovel, use it. If they hand you a pair of shears instead of electric hedge clippers, bite your lip and start scissoring. Don't ask questions. They have their reasons.

Normal people see

dirt.

Gardeners see

dormant

bulbs

mulch

earthworms

subsoil

topsoil

A whole universe.

3. Don't plant without permission. Yes, you know they love yellow roses. And, yes, you just found the most beautiful yellow rosebush known to man on sale at the nursery. By all means buy it. It is a wonderful gift! Just don't put it in the ground.

Do you know whether it needs sun or shade? Do you know where the sun and shade are in the garden? Do you know where every dormant bulb and rhizome lurks? Did you know they'd been saving that spot to put in a load of lilies?

Do you know where the deer like to browse, where the soil is best, where the tree roots suck up all the extra water? Even if you know *all* of that, there are probably a million other things you don't know. Buy the rose and offer to plant it, but don't plant it unless your gardener tells you exactly where to dig the hole. Or, better yet, don't buy them a rose at all. Because do you really know whether they adore yellow roses, or did you just overhear them gush in order to be polite to another gardener? The tastes of gardeners are specific and capricious. And that, my friend, is why God invented gift certificates.

4.Buy them chocolate. Do I need to elaborate? Chocolate is wonderful. Gardeners need it. Buy them some. Buy lots. Buy it in lots…

Activities to help your gardener grow strong

Making sure your gardener is healthy involves more than just taking care of their physical body. They need mental stimulation. For cats, you can provide this with a feather tied to the end of a string. For gardeners, it takes a little more planning, but there are plenty of easy activities you can arrange to keep their minds sharp.

Why you can't take gardeners to the movies.

Find egregious plant errors in movies.

Next time you manage to get your gardener to watch a movie or TV show, be alert to those scenes set outdoors. When one comes up, lean over to your gardener and ask, "Would those plants really grow in [insert movie location]?" Unless the scene is set in southern California, the answer should almost always be a resounding NO and your gardener will take great pleasure in leaning over and whispering in your ear, "*Agapanthus*? In Maine? Seriously? I mean, really!" Be aware that this risks driving the other moviegoers insane, so it is recommended you bring a large garden shovel in order to smack anyone who dares to order you to shut up and watch the movie.

Bulb bombing

The concept is simple: planting bulbs, be they crocuses, daffodils, or whatever else, in other people's gardens, or public spaces, without permission. It is a perfect activity because it allows your gardener to scope out spots in friends' gardens or neglected parks that would benefit from a dose of spring beauty, order the necessary bulbs, and creep around at dusk, furtively digging holes, inserting bulbs, and swiftly replacing the dirt to effectively conceal their subterfuge. Once the bulbs are in place, the gardener spends all winter in anticipation. Then, come spring, they experience the pleasure of casually visiting the bulb-bombing sites, and cackling with glee as people comment on how lovely the flowers are and wonder where on earth they came from. Best of all, it keeps your gardener busy playing in the dirt without their shoving still more plants into spaces that were completely full five years ago.

Troubleshooting Your Gardener

It is always distressing when your gardener breaks down or starts to malfunction. Often these problems will work themselves out over time, so be patient. A winter dormancy can often act as a hard reset, and a gardener will emerge in the spring realizing that trying to grow oranges in Minnesota is ridiculous, or that magenta really has no place in most color schemes. But sometimes the problems are more involved, and you'll need to take action to treat them.

Garden paralysis

The symptoms of garden paralysis are easy to spot. An ornamental grass bought as a small wisp in a gallon pot has ballooned to three feet across, filling what was once a well-used path and slashing viciously at the faces of every visitor. A vegetable garden that once produced bushels of produce has become shadier and shadier as trees matured around it, and now barely manages to squeeze out a single ripe tomato a year. What was once a narrow stream of fall anemones snaking through the garden has widened first into a river and then a flood, overwhelming countless helpless plants in its path. The big planter by the front step has been filled with the same pink petunias every spring for so many years that even the bees are bored by them.

To survive, gardeners must adapt as plants grow, trees expand, and tastes evolve. But in a case of garden paralysis, nothing changes. Aggressive perennials continue to spread, unchecked, and the same boring tomato varieties appear in the vegetable garden year after year. In a mild case, all your gardener needs is a kick-start. Treat the gardener to a shopping spree at a terrific nursery, and when they come home with a carload of new plants, they'll be forced to change something in order to find room for them. And, usually, once they dig up one bed, they reconsider all the others.

Yet, some gardens become so paralyzed that even a shopping trip fails to get them moving. In these serious cases, your best and simplest option is to hire a local construction crew to come over with a make-believe work order from the town to do something to your sewer line, or foundation—anything that requires a lot of digging. Have them flag out a proposed work area, which should galvanize your gardener to frantically start lifting all the plants in that area and transplanting them into pots in order to save them. Once the plants are out of the ground, have your construction friends come by one day with a bunch of shovels and pretend to work for a while, and, *hey, presto!* your gardener will be presented with a blank slate they can't resist and must redesign.

If you can't find anyone willing to put on an orange vest and dig holes, a less effective option is to buy a bottle of herbicide and spray it over the worst of the overgrown perennials. This not only eliminates a problem plant, but also creates a dead spot your gardener will have to replant. Be careful, however, and wait to spray plants in the late summer, just before they naturally go dormant for the fall, so your gardener won't realize they've been poisoned and grow hysterical. Instead, they will just think they mysteriously didn't make it through the winter.

You can also try leaving fake notes from the neighbors or Home Owners Association complaining about the moribund design or hire a professional garden designer to come out and consult. In short, whatever you have to do to get the garden moving, do it. A paralyzed garden is a dead garden.

Selective speech and hearing loss

Did the last sentence your gardener spoke sound something like, *"Platycodon Ranunculus Echinocereus reichenbachii caespitosus Clematis"*? Have they stopped using the words "leaves" and "flowers," replacing them with "bloom" and "foliage"? Have you ever caught them using the word "geophyte" when talking about crocuses and cyclamen because "bulb" isn't quite accurate? When was the last time you heard them speak a regular English word like "movie" or "music"? Your gardener may be suffering from selective speech loss, where they lose their ability to say anything that is not related to plants and gardening. This condition is common, serious, and often accompanied by selective hearing loss, where the gardener can no longer perceive sentences that don't include botanical Latin or phrases like, "Let's go to the nursery" or, "There are rabbits in the garden."

I've got bad news, and there is no point in sugar-coating it: There is no cure, no treatment, and nothing you can do. Your only hope is to learn Latin, for sometimes if you say, "*Lavare acetabula*" instead of "Wash the dishes," the Latin words trick their brain into hearing and paying attention before they realize that the particular Latin phrase you uttered doesn't refer to a plant.

Shopping addiction

If you've lived with a gardener for any length of time, you've no doubt seen the signs. And if the world of gardening is new to you, you will—sadly—see it soon. Boxes labeled "Live Plants! Protect from Heat and Freezing!" are delivered nearly daily. You leave for an afternoon and come back to catch your gardener in the act of feverishly planting a dozen new perennials, intent on fooling you into believing once they are in the ground that they have been there all along. You log onto Facebook and see your gardener posting a selfie featuring them grinning behind the wheel of a rental van packed to the ceiling with plants.

Obsessive plant shopping is one of the hardest things to deal with, and everyone who loves a gardener will come face to face with it sooner or later. The problem has only gotten worse in the modern world of social media, where the addict can find a circle of virtual gardener friends to cheer them on in their reckless obsession. There is no reasoning with the gardener, no way you'll convince them to stick to a budget. You need to resort to subterfuge. Sneak attacks. Low, underhanded tricks. Don't worry, it's easier than you think.

Start out by finding a comfortable seat by a window where you can see the mailbox. Watch it like a hawk. When you see the mail carrier appear, sprint outside and grab the mail. Quickly sort through the day's haul. Anything with a picture of a pretty flower on the cover goes straight into the trash. It doesn't matter whether it's a catalog, a flier from your local nursery, or a magazine full of plant photos that your gardener will instantly decide they "need." It doesn't even have to be gardening-related. As an added precaution, keep a pot of hot oatmeal on the stove, and upend it in the bin atop the plant porn so as to disguise it and prevent your gardener from rooting through the trash to recover their stash. Leaving a nice bar of dark chocolate on the counter also serves as an effective (if temporary) distraction.

Intercepting the mail is a temporary solution at best. After a few months, your gardener will almost certainly grow suspicious, requiring you to finesse your technique. Rather than discard all plant catalogs, let some of the crappy ones through, and throw away only the most dangerous. (Plant Delights and Annie's Annuals should be on the top of your destroy list.) Never let your gardener get their grubby little hands on these. The catalogs you can safely let through are those with Photoshopped "blue" roses or "20% OFF SALE!!!" splashed all over the cover – catalogs so trashy they'll merely depress your gardener rather than sending them into a shopping spasm.

I must caution you that limited access to the mail is only part of the battle. The internet still beckons with seductive catalogs. Some of the worst, in fact, can only be found online, and it goes without saying that a gardener can still visit nurseries in person with devastating results even if they never get the fliers, coupons, or announcements of season-end clearance sales.

If you have begged, pleaded, lied, and schemed and still

your gardener continues to shop wildly, your only option may be to get them hooked on seeds.

This may seem counterintuitive, but when there is no cure for the addiction, your only option is to find the safest, lowest-cost way to feed that addiction, and for gardeners, seeds can serve as the nicotine chewing gum they are still addicted to but keeps them from smoking. The most obvious reason you should encourage this is because seeds are cheap. A wild splurge on seeds will cost a mere fraction of a similar shopping binge on potted perennials. But, that is just the beginning; growing from seed isn't difficult, but it is a little more time consuming. And more time is a good thing, as idle hands are the nurseryman's playground. When your gardener buys a plant, they simply dig a hole, plop in the plant, water, and they're done. Seeds need to be sown, pricked out, fussed over while small, potted on to larger containers, perhaps moved to a nursery bed to grow before being moved out into their final location in the garden. Seeds keep the gardener busy, and when your gardener is busy, they don't have time to go shopping. Even better, one packet of seeds can easily produce dozens of plants, and more plants will get you to the magical point of a full garden faster. Be aware though that just because there is no room in the garden, that doesn't mean your gardener will stop shopping for more plants, but it does usually slow them down. When buying that new plant means ripping out an old one to make room, it forces the gardener to proceed with a little more caution.

To get your gardener hooked on seeds, start by building a raised bed, filling it with high-quality potting soil, and calling it a "seed bed." Encourage the gardener to sow the seeds of perennials and hardy annuals there, in the fall, and watch them get all excited when the seeds germinate in the spring and are soon ready for transplant elsewhere in the garden. Once they've gotten hooked on the ease of starting seeds in their seedbed, they're ready to graduate to a bank of lights and a small fan to start seeds indoors.

Magic.

Now available in a pack of seeds.

Getting your gardener to grow their plants from seed is, in many ways, a magic solution, but be aware that this treatment can result in some serious complications. The worst of these is when the gardener looks at all their lovely plants grown from seed and thinks, "I should start a nursery!" They'll argue that selling some plants makes sense and will offset the cost of their hobby, but don't be fooled. It will only lead to bad things, such as greenhouse purchasing, working twelve or fourteen hours a day, long rants about insane customers, and broken marriages. Head off any urge to start a nursery at all cost. If your gardener is boasting about their ability to grow anything and everything from seed, sneak in and gently mist a few choice seed pots with herbicide. A little unexplained seedling death will punch a nice hole in their nursery-craving ego. If all else fails, buy them a copy of Tony Avent's book, *So You Want to Start a Nursery?* This will give them a solid dose of reality and scare all but the most determined away from the nursery business. If, after all that, they still want to start a nursery, your only choice is to accept it and go back to school to become an accountant or get a MBA, so you can at least attempt to make the resulting business the rarest of all nurseries: one that actually turns a profit.

Parasites of gardeners

Just as there are aphids in the garden intent on sucking the roses dry, there are plenty of pests and parasites equally intent on taking advantage of your gardener. These include the fertilizer manufacturers that insist their product makes plants grow twice as big, the self-appointed Facebook garden gurus who pretend that Epsom salts should be used in the garden, and the marketers of little bottles of mysterious, unidentified "minerals and hormones" that claim to make plants overall grow "better."

The bigger the claim, the less it acvtually does

Less disease!

Kills insects!

Bigger plants!

Brings parrots back to life!

Wow STUFF!

Actually does: Nothing

If used properly controls powdery mildew

Actually does: Control powdery mildew

The best treatment for these parasites is actual, scientifically based information. State extension agencies throughout the United States produce oodles of wonderful fact sheets, which provide solutions proven to be effective against most parasites. Insisting that your gardener get a soil test before adding any fertilizers or other products to their soil will further steer them away from generic fertilizers packed with things their soil doesn't need (and doesn't want) and toward products that indeed help the garden to grow better. Finally, if they do want to try some wacky product, insist that they do a proper test, not merely spraying the whole garden down, but, rather, treating some plants and leaving others alone in a mini comparative trial so they can see whether the product does or (more likely) doesn't work.

The Tyranny of Spring

This is a common problem for all gardeners, especially in more northerly climates. In the mad rush of emotion and energy that is spring, they sprint out to the garden center and nursery and buy up every plant with a flower showing. All the great late-summer- and fall-blooming plants look dull and flowerless that time of year so most gardeners just breeze on past them. Then, in the calmer seasons of summer and fall, they are busy maintaining and harvesting vegetables, and never make it back to the nursery. This spring-only shopping results in a severely lopsided garden, full of plants that look terrific during the spring and early summer but boring and lifeless for the rest of the growing season. Vegetable gardeners have their own version of this, busily planting away from the earliest peas and lettuces through the tomatoes, peppers, and eggplants while overlooking planting fall crops of broccoli or turnips or greens.

Now, you may admit the truth of this but not think it matters, but let me promise you – it matters a lot. If the garden is only interesting in the spring, the gardener gets bored as the season goes on, gardening less and less, which eventually launches them into severe garden withdrawal and all the horrible problems that entails, early in the winter. You need to keep your gardener as busy as possible and happy and delighted with the garden right up to the first snowfall—even after, if you can manage it. You need them to end the year on a big dose of flowery, fresh vegetable-y joy so it can tide them through the first few weeks of winter.

The tyranny of spring is pervasive and harder to break than you might imagine. It's a bit of a vicious cycle as nurseries and garden centers no longer keep good things in stock the rest of the year for the very reason that many gardeners only shop in the spring. If your gardener tries to shop in the summer and fall, they'll likely find slim pickings, which makes them not want to shop, which means the garden centers keep even less plants around the following year. It is a vicious cycle. And every nurseryman knows that most people will buy twenty plants in bloom for every one they pick up that is out of flower, so stocking a lot of great fall-blooming plants is pretty much a waste of time.

There are solutions, however—ways to rebel against

spring's hegemony. First, haul your gardener off to lots of other gardens during the summer and fall. Visit really great public gardens, or beg a chance to see the personal gardens of some talented local plant people. While you are there, take lots and lots of pictures of anything that looks exceptionally good in the latter part of the year. Then, come winter, pull out those pictures and set your gardener to researching every plant shown so that next spring, they can be sure to buy good summer and fall performers, even though those plants probably won't look like much during the spring shopping season. When your gardener puts in a long row of *Lespedeza thunbergii* that explodes in waterfalls of vivid pink flowers at the end of summer, they'll love it so much they will likely become addicted to tracking down other really terrific plants that bloom at the same time. The result is a more balanced garden, a longer season of pleasure, and yet another task to absorb your gardener and keep them busy researching over the long winter months.

Support organizations

Caring for a gardener is not unlike gardening: it can be a lot of work. Putting up with their endless babble of Latin names, worry about the weather and all the other little oddities and difficulties inherent in dealing with this bizarre and obsessive type of person can sometimes be too much. Luckily, you don't have to, and shouldn't, try to do it alone. It may take a village to raise a child, but it takes a plant society to raise a gardener.

Gardening can be an isolating passion, work done alone, at home, with a bunch of voiceless plants. If your gardener quietly works away talking to no one, it is not a good situation. You need to take steps to get them involved with a community of gardeners right away. And, no, while all those Facebook groups they keep joining are better than nothing, they aren't enough.

The benefits to being part of a garden club or plant society are numerous. Besides the obvious psychological benefits of talking to other humans, interacting with fellow gardeners will take some of the pressure off you, the normal person. When your gardener gets to spend an entire evening talking about nothing but plants with a bunch of other plant-obsessed people, they may have gotten their fix and be able to spend some time talking about something else, possibly even something that you, the non-gardener, cares about. Possibly. Well, I wouldn't count on it, but there is just the tiniest of chances. And there are other, more reliable benefits as well. Gardeners are generous souls by nature, and once your gardener starts to hang out with them, they will come home with armloads of free plants. Your household budget will rejoice. Even better, when your gardener divides a beloved perennial, instead of trying to force all the divisions into beds already groaning because there's no room left, all because they can't quite bear to otherwise throw them in the compost pile, they can now slip those spare plants into leftover nursery pots and haul them off to their next meeting, where they will go to good loving homes and be appreciated.

Another huge plus is the opportunity to learn from others' experiences. A solitary gardener is likely to go out on a limb and order whole collections of cool-sounding perennials only to have them all die the first winter. A gardener in a garden club or plant society can ask around and find out if this particular plant simply doesn't do well in your climate, thereby saving untold amounts of money and grief.

For all these benefits, it must be admitted there are drawbacks as well. The meetings often involve talks and tours where your gardener will learn about amazing plants that they just *must* add to next year's shopping list, and when they hear about other gardener's successes, it encourages them to try even more new plants. But, despite that, the net effect on the household budget more often than not is a positive one.

Even better, being part of a garden organization gives the gardener something to do, something that doesn't involve buying more plants or expanding the garden yet again. Make sure whatever organization they join has a big meeting in the dead of winter, and if it doesn't, encourage them to start one, so that your gardener will get sucked into organizing and keep as busy as can be during the snowed-in months. The key to this being effective is to jolt your gardener out of their mundane role as one of various people who show up to meetings and into becoming one of the Same Ten People. If you've ever been part of a small club or society, you know about the Same Ten People. It is always the Same Ten People who organize every event, put out the newsletter, serve as president, secretary, treasurer, and dog catcher. The Same Ten People do everything while the rest of the group just shows up at meetings when they feel like it—no responsibility, no accountability. Once you succeed in motivating your gardener to become one of the Same Ten People, they'll instantly be so busy that you'll never have to worry about them again.

Luckily, it is easy to move into the ranks of the Same Ten People. One of the Same Ten People is always about to die, or move to Florida, or give up gardening and become one of the Same Ten People for the American Terrier Society. Faced with the prospect of becoming an insignificant nine, the Same Ten People are always on the prowl for replacements. Being drafted is easy. Anyone who shows up to every meeting—especially if they are early—is a prime target. Then all it takes is to agree to any seemingly small task. Setting up chairs for the meeting morphs into helping with the newsletter just this once, which becomes serving as secretary (it takes no time at all; we just need someone to do it!), and before you know it, your gardener is president, then ex-president, runs the plant sale, and is so busy they have to quit their job so they can focus all their time and energy on making sure the society works perfectly, while complaining that no one else contributes. You, meanwhile, get to relax at home and hang out with normal people, confident your gardener is too busy to get into trouble.

Finding a good gardening organization can be a challenge, and this is where you, as the caregiver of a gardener, may need to do some investigative work. Gardening organizations, from garden clubs to plant societies, are hanging on by a thread in many places, often being killed off by ridiculous practices. Too many garden clubs meet on a Tuesday at 10 a.m., efficiently excluding anyone with a job from attending, and too many others spend an hour on tedious business meetings, taking minutes and following strict Roberts Rules of Order, rather than getting to the core of what makes for a great gardening meeting. A good garden organization needs fertilizer, namely lots of chocolate, an assortment of adult beverages, extra plants and seeds for members to share, enthusiastic informal plant chatter, and a brief, fun, informative presentation about plants with oodles of pictures to get everyone salivating over cool plants.

If you can find an organization that is run well, drive your gardener there and watch them thrive. More than likely, however, you will send your gardener to a meeting only to have them come home depressed, and asking why anyone needs these things now that we have the internet. In that case, you need to step in and reform your local club or society in order to create a habitat where your gardener can thrive. First, contact the group's president, offer to help with refreshments, and bring a couple of bottles of wine. (Plus chocolate, of course.) Next, sneak onto your gardener's email and social media accounts, track down every gardener they know in the area, and bully them all into attending the meeting the same day, thereby overwhelming the boring old school garden clubbers by sheer force of numbers. Then, start whittling away at the boring business meeting format, the long-winded speakers, and the inconvenient meeting time, and before you know it you'll have transformed the stuffy, moribund garden club into a rich, fun, satisfying part of your gardener's life. That's when you can bow out, leave the gardeners to nurture the seeds that you have sown, and relax at home doing whatever it is non-gardeners do with their time.

Subspecies and Varieties of Gardeners

If you think all gardeners are the same, you are sadly mistaken. The disease of gardening can take many different paths and latch onto myriad aspects of the wide world of growing plants. Some of these types of gardeners are easier to live with and handle than others, ranging from the odd to the outright obnoxious. We'll talk though some of the most common varieties of gardeners so you can more precisely identify the gardener in your life, understand the best ways to care for them, and get some ideas on how to treat the most objectionable of their habits.

The Nativist

This particular obsession often comes on slowly. It starts with your gardener reading a book about interesting native insects, volunteering for a day to pull some invasive weedy species from a local park, or mentioning how under appreciated some obscure genus of native wild flowers is. The next thing you know, they've ripped out the one border you actually liked—the one with the roses and lilies—and turned it into a "prairie" that looks for all the world like a bunch of roadside weeds run amok.

Though sometimes, in the early stages of nativist gardening, the results can be not very garden like, there are a lot of wonderful things. That garden of native plants is ecologically sensetive and a have for beautiful butterflies and song birds, and by eschewing any plant that originated more than six feet from their garden, it is much harder for the nativist to go on mad shopping binges, as they refuse to purchase the majority of plants available for sale at their local garden center or nursery.

On the downside, that love of native plants of supporting the local ecology can develop in very unpleasant ways. Like dandelions sprouting amid the *Rudbeckia* and *Echinacea*, strains of thoroughly unpleasant judgmental self-righteousness all too often spring up in the nativist garden. Left unchecked, your gardener will start alienating most of their gardener friends.

Your best tool is the wealth of scientific research which indicates that while including a wide diversity of plants, especially natives, in your garden is a great way to provide suitable habitat for native insects and animals, the vast majority of non-native plants are not harmful to the large ecosystem, with the exception of a few species which have been shown to be truly invasive and damaging. Guide your gardener to think in terms of adding native plants to the garden rather than replacing, which requires having to rip out every other plant in the ground. This will enable you to enjoy a garden that is both lovely and ecologically responsible, and take the edge off their self-righteousness.

The Designer

Does your gardener spend hours at the nursery holding different plants next to each other, trying to find just the right combination? Do they use words like "lavender" or "coral" instead of "purple" and "pink" to describe flower colors, or, even worse, modify every color description with words like "warm" or "saturated"? Do they rip out an entire border in midsummer because the colors are all wrong? Do they drool over bluestone pavers and talk constantly about sight lines and focal points? If so, your gardener is a designer.

Let's start with the good news. You are going to live in absolute beauty. While most other gardeners surround you with a solid wall of wild, untamed greenery, a designer creates an exquisite work of art. Now the bad news: You will go broke. Designers won't settle for a six-pack of annuals—they buy them by the flat. And then another flat the following week because the first one wasn't quite the right shade of purple. They don't just get gravel for the walk; they spend four hours determining which gravel is exactly the right shade of gray, breezing past the fact that it would be cheaper to make paths literally out of gold. See that antique Italian terra cotta urn that costs $4,000? It's beautiful! Who cares what it costs?

There are a couple of ways to deal with a designer in your life. The first option is to win the lottery. Once a year. For the rest of your life. If you can't manage that, found a wildly successful tech startup and sell it to Google for a few billion dollars. If neither of those are an option, there are several tricks to control your designer. One is to introduce them to the world of "upcycling." Be sure you use the word upcycling, however, rather than simply "filling your garden with trash" or they probably won't go for it. The designer-turned-upcycler haunts thrift stores and yard sales, hauling home random finds to repurpose into planters and pavers and retaining walls. Though this method does run the risk of being, well, unspeakably ugly, a true designer can make something beautiful out of the "pre-owned materials" and even if you wind up living in a garden that looks like a dumpster exploded, you can take solace in the fact that your bank account remains intact.

Another approach is to take advantage of the fact that designers love to plan more than anything. They're never happier than when scheming away, so the goal is to trick them to spend more of their time planning than actually planting or building. A big drafting table is a good investment here, as they'll have so much fun drawing up designs that it won't leave them much time to follow through on them all. Once they've sketched out a million different plans and settled on The One, introduce them to the idea where you install the design in stages, implementing different sections every couple of years, to avoid breaking the bank all at once. Your designer will likely envision three or four stages. You should fight to divide it up into ten, or twenty, because there is one thing you can always count on: a designer always goes over budget. *Always.* So the trick here is to make that starting budget as small as possible. And bring lots of chocolate to the budget negotiations. It never fails to soften them up.

If nothing else works, there is only one thing to be done:

turn your designer loose on other people's gardens. Send them back to school to get a landscape architecture degree, if need be, but get them out there working as a designer and getting paid to spend other people's money on gardens. If they're really talented, they might even make a profit, but even if they only break even, that's a whole lot better than draining your bank account dry.

The Collector

You would think that a gardener would desire a plant because it is beautiful to look at or delicious to eat. That would make sense, right? That's the assumption often made by normal people, but when it comes to hard-core gardeners, things don't often make a lot of sense. There are masses of gardeners, the collectors, who want a plant only because it is unusual. And don't assume that unusual just means unusual looking. That is part of it, but many collectors simply want a plant that is rarely seen in gardens, even if it doesn't possess any attractive or useful features.

If your gardener is a collector, you'll have no trouble figuring it out. Collectors never use common names; they're inordinately proud of the fact that the plants they grow are too rare, too unusual, to have earned a common name, so the collector's conversation is a constant stream of Latin binomials. They never shop at regular garden centers because plants with big showy flowers or large, tasty fruits simply don't interest them. Another dead giveaway: the collector's garden is hideous, packed to the gills with more plants than there is space for. Many of the individual plants will, of course, be insanely beautiful, perfectly grown, and strikingly unusual, but there will be no sense of design, no color scheme, and, worst of all, never more than one of each type of plant. A collector's garden is consistently little more than a wild cacophony of diversity.

Normal Gardener:

Collector:

If your gardener is a collector, brace yourself. Many collectors end up confusing the concept of "desirable" with that of "expensive" and can max out credit cards faster than almost anyone.

How do I know so much about collectors? Well... let's just say I once spent long hours using automatic translation tools to manage to convince a nursery in Russia to send me seeds for a species of *Nonea* which boasts a weedy growth habit and small, uninteresting purple flowers simply because I had never seen that particular species grown before. It is safe to say I know what I'm talking about here.

Your best strategy when dealing with a collector is to divide the space you have in two parts—one part, somewhere out in the back, out of the public eye, as a collector bed where they can just put all their oddities in rows with no pretension toward design, while the rest of the garden is designated as ornamental beds, where they may only plant things that truly look attractive and only in large enough numbers that they don't look ridiculous. This will allow the collector to indulge their fetish for freaky oddities without drowning you in a sea of ugliness. As a bonus, this also furnishes less room for their weird collections, forcing them to limit themselves to only those plants they love best, which limits their wild shopping extravagances, at least to some degree.

This scheme of dividing the garden between collection

and ornamental display is a great one, except for one big flaw: it probably won't work. The true collector may well agree to it, but as soon as the collector bed is full, you are sure to come out one day and catch them kneeling in the display bed, putting in a lily they excitedly tell you is the only member of the genus that reliably produces tiny, ugly, green flowers. It is a losing battle. But you might as well try.

The "just one genus"

These are the blinkered gardeners who somehow have fallen hard for one group of plants, leaving them oblivious to the remaining glorious horticultural universe. These are the people who fill an entire garden with hostas and refuse to consider adding so much as a single fern for a little diversity and interest, or fill the house with grow lights and orchids while the outdoor garden is a dismal spread of weedy lawn.

The just-one-genus folks go nuts for a daylily with flowers a color that is a sorry excuse for washed out lavender, calling it "blue" while ignoring the fact that there are delphiniums and salvia and countless other true blue flowers they could grow instead. They plant twelve identical hostas and hallucinate differences between them just because some hosta "breeder" has decided to give a new name to the same old green plant with a white edge to its leaves.

If this describes the gardener in your life, do not give up hope. I was one of these gardeners. Early in my gardening career, I had a grand, wild passion for roses. Swept away be velvety fragrant petals, my love was blind to the black spot and thorns and the fact that all other plant existed. I craved roses, only roses, willfully turning my back on every other lovely plant in the world.

I still have what can only be called a deeply irrational love for roses, growing them despite the fact that they are mostly awkward disease-ridden plants, but my love is no longer exclusive. The cure was nothing more than a packet of snapdragon seeds I picked up on a whim. When the snapdragons began blooming, it just took one good look and I realized that they were both beautiful and not roses. What if there were other beautiful, non-rose plants? I would have to grow them all and find out.

So take your hosta obsessive or iris freak out to a good nursery and tell them you will pay for the whole shopping trip provided they buy three plants outside their preferred genus. Yes, they'll grumble and complain, but then just watch as they pick up a fern or daylily or baptisia and suddenly realize there is a whole glorious world out there they have been ignoring all these years.

Food, food, oh glorious food

It seems great, at first, having a food-obsessed gardener. Even in the late winter when they take over the entire house with grow lights to start their tomato seedlings, it might seem okay. Sure, the electric bill is through the roof, but vegetable seeds are inexpensive, and you get a lot of delicious food out of it. But later in the gardening season, when you've been forced to eat seventeen pounds of zucchini a day in a mad attempt to keep up with what the garden produces, the house is a million degrees because the air conditioning can't cope with all the heat generated by their canning, roasting, and dehydrating, they come home with a sixth chest freezer for the basement, and when people come to visit, they have to crawl on hands and knees to enter the guest room to avoid whacking their head on all the garlic and onions hanging from the ceiling to dry, the charm kinda wears thin.

The first step to dealing with your foodie gardener is to get rid of excess produce. Your friends are already ducking you because they don't want any more damn cucumbers, but your local food bank or homeless shelter should welcome you with open arms. The program Plant a Row for the Hungry facilitates these kinds of gardener produce donations. Connect your foodie with them to take some of the pressure off your stomach and the six overflowing freezers.

Next, channel some of that food-growing energy into something that you won't have to eat, can, freeze, or otherwise deal with. You'll never get a hard-core food grower to dive straight into a mixed herbaceous border, but you often can lure them in the direction of growing non-edibles by way of cut flowers. Start them off with something straightforward, like zinnias. Your gardener can sow the big seeds in rows like they would their carrots and harvest the flowers just like they do their zucchini. And even if they get bit by the cut-flower bug and grow so many zinnias and cosmos and dahlias and gladioli that your house is full, a big armload of fresh flowers is always a welcome gift (unlike an armload of zucchini). All your friends who had started lying about being out of town all summer to avoid the unwelcome vegetable deluge will suddenly reappear and start inviting you over for parties just to get their hands on some of the beautiful blooms.

Final Thoughts

Living with a gardener can be difficult. Being temporarily widowed every spring, when they haven't time to sleep much less talk to you, getting dragged off to gardens when you'd rather be visiting museums or shopping, dealing with the endless stream of dirt they track into the house, listening, once again, to why they do or do not believe worm castings live up to the hype, sharing your closets, basement, and driveway with the ever-expanding wave of plants and lights and seeds, and having your prized Egyptian cotton sheets whisked off your bed and onto the garden bed to ward off frost isn't easy.

As one of the most extreme gardeners out there, I offer my condolences and apologies. In our defense, may I just argue that along with all the dirt and mayhem we gardeners stir up, we also sincerely try to make the world a more beautiful place than it would otherwise be without us? We work that subtlest of magic, the one that transforms a patch of earth and a handful of tiny brown seeds into brilliant flowers and juicy, sun-warmed fruit. And if living with a gardener is proving too much for you, despite all the sage advice sprinkled across these pages, there is one solution that works every time. It's a magic bullet to stop you from feeling resentment when you return from every vacation with your luggage full of plants that smear mud on your clothes, or at how your car reeks of that load of manure your gardener coaxed you to transport from the guy with the horses up the street.

The answer is simple. Become a gardener.

Go on, step outside and turn over a bit of warm, brown soil and let it filter through your fingers. Tuck a dahlia tuber or tomato seedling into the ground, and watch the magic of gardening at work. Step back and be amazed at how misshapen brown lumps and a few slender green threads transform themselves into vigorous beauty and sustenance. Feel your way into the irrational love of plants, and, along with your gardener, create a little paradise, as perfect a garden as can be, and ignore how it looks like pure madness to the "normal" people on the outside looking in.

C'mon. Join us.

34521148R00060

Made in the USA
San Bernardino, CA
03 May 2019